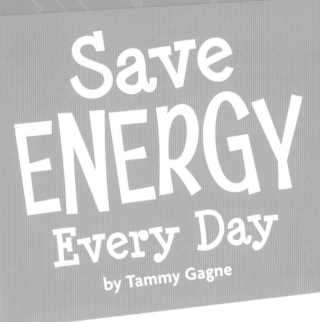

Save ENERGY Every Day

by Tammy Gagne

amicus
high interest

Amicus High Interest is published by Amicus
P.O. Box 1329, Mankato, MN 56002
www.amicuspublishing.us

Library of Congress Cataloging-in-Publication Data
Gagne, Tammy.
  Save energy every day / Tammy Gagne.
     pages cm. -- (Kids save the Earth)
  Includes bibliographical references and index.
  ISBN 978-1-60753-518-8 (hardcover) -- ISBN 978-1-60753-549-2 (eBook)
  1. Energy conservation--Juvenile literature. I. Title.
  TJ163.35.G324 2013
  644--dc23
                                   2013008497

Photo Credits: Shutterstock Images, cover, 2, 5, 6, 19, 22; Red Line
Editorial, 8, 15; iStockphoto, 11; Thinkstock, 12; Mike Flippo/Shutterstock
Images, 17; Sony Ho/Shutterstock Images, 20

Produced for Amicus by The Peterson Publishing Company
and Red Line Editorial.

Editor Jenna Gleisner
Designer Becky Daum
Printed in the United States of America
Mankato, MN
July, 2013
PA 1938
10 9 8 7 6 5 4 3 2 1

TABLE OF CONTENTS

WHAT IS ENERGY?

We use **energy** every day. It gives us heat. It powers our cars. It turns on our TVs, lights, and computers. Energy comes from many places. It can come from sunlight, water, and wind.

5

USING ENERGY

Most energy comes from coal, oil, and **natural gas**. Earth takes millions of years to make them. We might use them up before more is made. They will last longer if we save energy.

Let's Do It

Put in new compact fluorescent lightbulbs. They use less power. And they last 25 times longer than old ones.

How a Power Plant Works

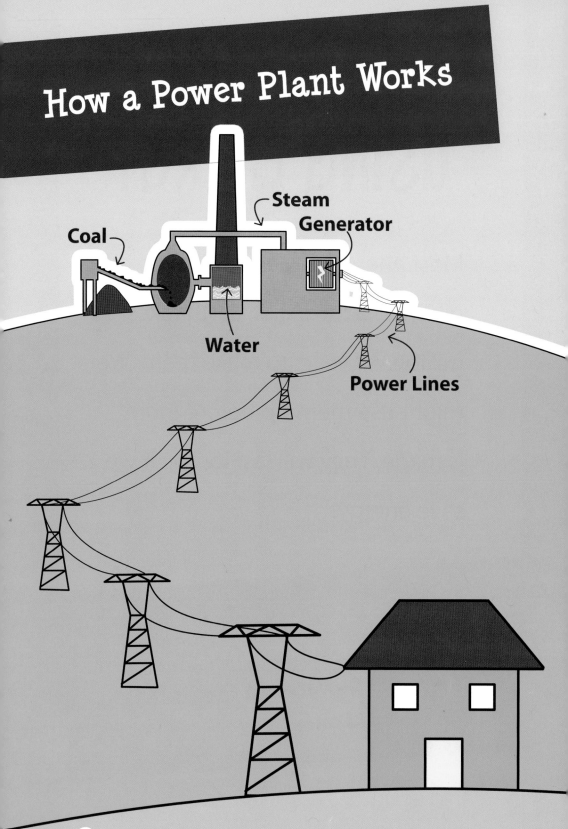

Steam

Generator

Coal

Water

Power Lines

HOW WE GET ENERGY

A **power plant** makes coal into energy. The coal is burned. It heats water. This makes steam. Steam turns a **generator** to make energy. Then the energy goes to power lines that reach our homes.

TURN OFF MACHINES

You can help save energy. Machines use a lot of it. Watch less TV. Read a book. Or ask a friend to play. What is a game you can play?

Let's Do It

When you turn off a video game, it still uses power. All the little lights take power. Unplug it!

SUN POWER

Use power from the sun. Open
a window shade on sunny days.
The sun will light your room. It
can help heat your home, too.
Let warm sunlight in. The heater
will use less power.

WIND POWER

Wind turbines use wind to make power. They are very tall. They catch more wind up high. Wind turns the long blades. They spin a generator to make power.

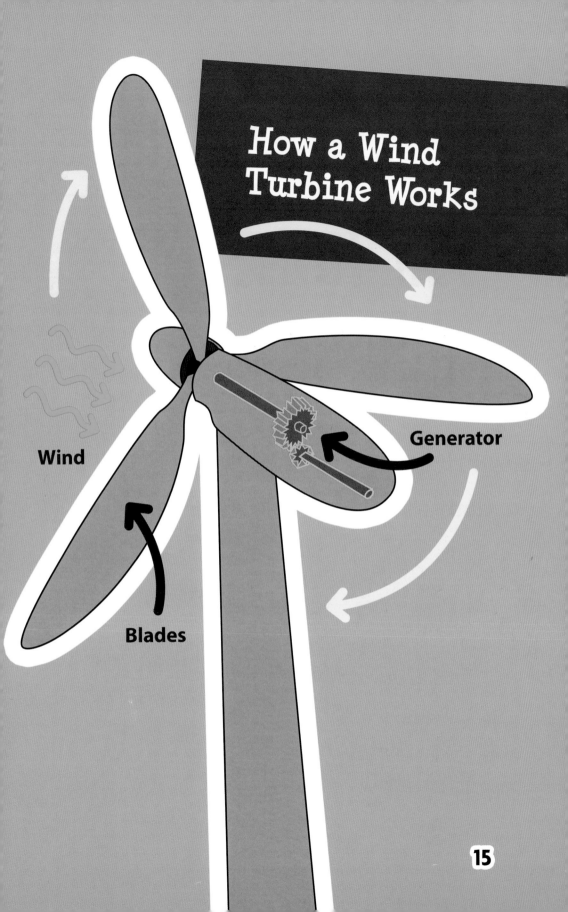

How a Wind Turbine Works

Wind

Generator

Blades

SAVE ENERGY AT HOME

You can use wind power at home. Use the wind to dry your clothes. Hang them on a clothesline.

Let's Do It

See if your window has a leak. Hold your hand where it closes. Tell a parent if you feel air. Then you can help fix it.

SAVE ENERGY AT SCHOOL

We can save energy at school.
Have a contest. See which class can
come up with the most ideas to
save power.

Let's Do It

Turn off the light if your class leaves
a room. Power down computers at
the end of the day.

$1 \times 4 = 4$

$2 \times 4 = 8$

$3 \times 4 = 12$

$4 \times 4 = 16$

$4 \times 5 = 20$

$4 \times 6 = 24$

$4 \times 7 =$

$4 \times$

4

SAVE GAS

Do you get a ride to school? Set up a **car pool**. Parents can take turns driving. Then only one car has to drive. Walk or ride your bike. It will save gas.

These are just some ways to save energy. What are your ideas?

21

GET STARTED TODAY

- Turn off lights when you leave a room.

- Open window shades for light.

- Layer up on chilly days.

- Cut down on TV time.

- Walk or ride your bike to save gas.

- Plan a lights-out night.

WORDS TO KNOW

car pool – a group of people that ride together in one car

compact fluorescent lightbulbs – lightbulbs that save energy and last a long time

energy – power that can be used

generator – a machine that makes electricity

natural gas – a gas found under the ground or ocean that is used for fuel

power plant – a station where electrical power is made and sent out

wind turbines – tall structures with long blades that turn in the wind to make electricity

LEARN MORE

Books

Antill, Sara. *10 Ways I Can Save the Earth*. New York: PowerKids Press, 2012.

Chambers, Catherine. *Go Green! Lead the Way*. New York: Crabtree, 2011.

Web Sites

Energy Hog
http://energyhog.org/childrens.htm
Find the energy hogs in your home.

Energy Star Kids
http://www.energystar.gov/index.cfm?c=kids.kids_index
Become an Energy Star with tips to help save energy in your home.

Kids Saving Energy
http://www1.eere.energy.gov/kids/
Learn more ways to help save energy.

INDEX